CW00373288

RAIL 8 PORTFOLIOS

The 24s and 25s

Hugh Dady

First published 1989

ISBN 0 7110 1846 4

All rights reserved. No part of this book may be reproduced or transmitted in any form or by any means, electronic or mechanical, including photocopying, recording or by any information storage and retrieval system, without permission from the Publisher in writing.

© Ian Allan Ltd 1989

Published by

IAN ALLAN LTD

Terminal House Shepperton TW17 8AS
Telephone: Walton-on-Thames (0932) 228950
Fax: 0932 232366   Telex: 929806 IALLAN G
Registered Office: Terminal House Shepperton TW17 8AS
Printed by Butler & Tanner Ltd, Frome and London

Front cover: Class 25/2 No 25120 passes Dent signalbox and nears the station, the highest in England, with a Bescot-Carlisle mixed freight. No 25120, outshopped from Derby Works as No D5270 in 1964, had a 19-year career on BR, ending its days working out of Crewe depot before withdrawal following accident damage in November 1983. *John S. Whiteley*
Pentax SP1000 85mm Takumar Kodachrome 25

Back cover: The first 'baby Sulzer' to be preserved was Class 24 No D5032. Following sale to private contractor J. T. Thompson for scrapping, it was loaned to the North Yorkshire Moors Railway which was unable to run steam because of the 1976 drought. To this day it remains on the line and has been named *Helen Turner* after the daughter of the director of the owning company. On 4 June 1983 No D5032 leaves Grosmont with the 16.55 for Pickering. *Hugh Dady*
Nikkormat FT2 50mm Nikkor Kodachrome 64
1/250, f4.5

Right: The depot building at Exeter provides an attractive frame for No 25274 on 3 May 1975. *Norman Preedy*
Pentax Spotmatic Agfa CT18

Introduction

The 478 Sulzer Type 2s were at one time second only to the Brush Type 4s in numerical strength. There were 151 of the 1,160bhp variety, later designated Class 24 and 327 of the later 1,250bhp Class 25 variant. The Class 24s employed the Sulzer 6LDA28-A power unit while the '25s' used the 'B' variant giving a slightly higher power output.

To some extent, the locomotives represented an echo of the 'small engine' policy of the Midland Railway, for they were to work both branch and main line duties either singly or in pairs. The majority were built at Derby, but Crewe and Darlington shared in their construction and in addition there were those privately contracted to the Beyer Peacock works at Gorton.

Between them these classes literally spanned the country, from Great Yarmouth to Holyhead and from Thurso to Penzance. Perhaps lacking the glamour of the more powerful types, their guttural rasping sound seemed an inseparable part of the BR scene.

In the late 1960s BR's traction fleet was critically examined with a view to eliminating the less successful classes and reducing the multiplicity of types which the modernisation plan had produced. The National Traction Plan spelt the end for the Class 24s although the last example in capital stock, No 24081, was to last until October 1980. Meanwhile the Class 25s spread their wings and helped to oust several non-standard types including Classes 17, 22

and 29. The recession of 1980/81 was the spur to start withdrawals of Class 25s and condemnations started in earnest. By the end of 1981 there were 205 locomotives left and this figure had dropped to 100 at the end of 1984.

Like all diesels, the Sulzer Type 2s had their faults, but with a life spanning 28 years they could certainly be considered as one of the better buys for BR. Their major shortcoming was the traction motors as the failure rate of those allocated to West Highland line duty demonstrated.

Little interest was shown by enthusiasts until their closing years. The repainting and naming of No 25322 and the later formation of Subclass 25/9, consisting of 12 examples specially designated to work mineral traffic in the northwest, provided some variety. Fortunately the distinctive Sulzer throb will continue to be heard as a considerable number of both Classes 24 and 25 have escaped the scrapyard. It is thanks to the preservationists that future generations will still be able to sample the familiar sight and sound of these machines which hauled so much traffic throughout Britain.

The compiler would like to thank the many photographers who submitted work for this project. I would also like to acknowledge the early work put in by Murray Brown when the volume was originally contracted by Jane's, and the help received from Chris Shaw at Ian Allan Ltd.

Hugh Dady
December 1988

Left: No less than six BR-Sulzer Type 2s can be seen in this view of Crewe Holding Sidings taken on 7 June 1979. Crewe was probably the area most strongly associated with these locomotives over the years, and the station environs always seemed to echo to the throaty Sulzer rasp. Compare the frontal design of the Class 24 on the right with the squarer profile of Class 25/2 No 25216 in the centre. This machine only had some 16 months of service left when the picture was taken, being withdrawn in December 1980 and cut up at Derby in March 1983. *Barry J. Nicolle*
Pentax SP2
50mm Takumar Agfa CT18 1/125, f8

Above: No D5000, the first of the BR Sulzer Type 2s, stands at its home depot of Willesden in May 1963. Completed at Derby in July 1958, the locomotive was displayed later that month at Marylebone before commencing trials over the Peak Forest route. Wilkes & Ashmore were the consultant designers and No D5000 was the only locomotive to carry the thin eggshell blue lining around the middle of the body. Later members carried a revised livery with off-white bands at gutter level and at the base of the body. When withdrawn as No 24005 at Reddish in January 1976, the National Railway Museum was advised of its availability, but wished, instead, to secure a Type 2

built by a private contractor and claimed the Brush Type 2 No D5500. No D5000 was scrapped at Swindon Works. *Geoff Rixon*
Pentax Kodachrome 2

Left: Sunday 18 June 1961, finds No D5020 trundling towards Hampton-in-Arden with a short parcels train — a working which would certainly not have taxed the locomotive unduly! Entering traffic in August 1959, this locomotive was destined to spend exactly 16 years in service, being withdrawn in August 1975 and cut up at Swindon Works in April 1977. At the time the picture was taken, the class were a common sight on the southern part of the London Midland Region engaged on all manner of secondary duties. *Michael Mensing*
Hasselblad 1000F 80mm Tessar Agfa CT18
1/1000, f3.2

Right: Of the first batch of 30 BR-Sulzer Type 2s, 15 were initially allocated to the Southern Region for mixed traffic work in the Chatham-Faversham-Dover area, as well as freight diagrams based on Hither Green. Their tasks included the heavy boat trains to the South Coast, one of which is seen here heading south through Sandling in the care of No D5018 on a fine June day in 1960. As deliveries of the Southern's 1,550hp Type 3s (later to become Class 33) progressed, the Type 2s were reallocated to the London Midland Region to perform the work for which they were originally intended.
The late Derek Cross

Right: Resplendent in green livery with small yellow warning panels, and with immaculate Mk 1 stock in tow, No D5085 is seen on the now-closed Rugby-Peterborough line at Market Harborough. The train is the 3.55pm Birmingham New Street-Yarmouth and the date is 4 June 1966, the last day of public service on this line.
Michael Mensing
Nikkorex F 50mm Nikkor Agfa CT18 1/500, f2.5

Right: Snowplough-fitted No D5114 shows a clean exhaust as it coasts past Cove Bay with the 5.25pm Aberdeen-Glasgow Buchanan Street on 5 July 1964. Nowadays a train of such length would be rostered for Type 4 motive power, but the timings of the 1960s were such that the operators in Scotland felt no need for such extravagance, the response to particularly heavy loads being double-heading with Type 2s. Derby-built No D5114 was one of only 14 Class 24s never to receive a five-digit number under the TOPS system, being withdrawn in October 1972 before the renumbering scheme came into effect. *Michael Mensing*
Nikkorex F 50mm Nikkor Agfa CT18
1/1000, f2.5

Right: No D5267 heads through the beautiful Hope Valley one mile north of Hope with a Chinley-Sheffield local on Whit Sunday, 17 May 1964. This was one of the locomotive's first workings. It spent all of its life on the London Midland Region and later became No 25117. Condemned in January 1984, the locomotive met its end at Swindon Works in May 1984. *Michael Mensing*
Voigtlander Bessa 11   High Speed Ektachrome 1/500, f3.2

Right: Many will feel that two-tone green was a particularly attractive livery. No D5282 lends weight to this view as it stands newly completed at Derby on 28 June 1964. It remained a Midland Region machine throughout its life. No 25132 was its TOPS number which it gained in February 1974. Swindon Works cut it up in November 1984, the loco having been withdrawn from Manchester Longsight on 20 December 1982. *Trevor Owen*
Leica M2   Kodachrome II

Right: A quarter of a century ago, this was the everyday sight on Tyneside — Sulzer Type 2s on local trip workings. Derby-built No D5149 was allocated to Gateshead when new in February 1961 and stayed on Tyneside until 1968. Photographed at Manors on 21 May 1962, this locomotive was never renumbered as a Class 24 as it was withdrawn at Glasgow in October 1972 and met its fate at Glasgow Works, then known as St Rollox.
Michael Mensing
Retina 2A   Ektachrome   1/500, f3.2

Left: A superb vintage scene at the north end of Leicester station sees No D7581 at the head of a down parcels train while BR-Sulzer Type 4 'Peak' No D90 approaches with a St Pancras-bound express. Note the wealth of period detail in this 11 May 1967 view, in particular the fine array of semaphores which lasted until the recent resignalling scheme. No D7581 was delivered new from Darlington in 1963, and enjoyed a 22-year career until its withdrawal as No 25231 on 23 August 1985. Ironically the locomotive was scrapped in Leicester, at Vic Berry's scrapyard.   *C. N. Banks*
Kodak Bantam   Kodachrome II

Left: Sporting its tell-tale trademark of a Glasgow Works repair (with the number on the bodyside instead of the cab side), No 24009 looks resplendent at Eastfield depot on 11 June 1975. This well travelled locomotive, despite its appearance and attention received, only lasted a further year in service and was one of several of its class to be dragged to Doncaster Works for disposal.
Norman Preedy
Pentax Spotmatic Agfa CT18

Right: A fine portrait of Class 24s Nos 24035 and 24081 at Crewe station preparing to work light to Stoke-on-Trent on 4 March 1978. Both machines were built at Crewe Works, the former in August 1959 and the latter in March 1960, and ended their BR days based at Crewe working a variety of secondary services. The rundown of the Class 24 fleet began in earnest in the mid-1970s but No 24081 was destined to outlast all its brethren by some 18 months, escaping withdrawal until October 1980. The locomotive is now preserved at Steamport Railway Museum, Southport. No 24035 was less fortunate, being cut up at Doncaster Works in December 1978. *Barry J. Nicolle*
Pentax SP2 Agfa CT18 1/125, f5.6-8

Above: The Class 25s have always been noted for their versatility, making them ideal for short-notice, non-diagrammed turns such as inspection trains, permanent way duties and attending breakdowns. No D7674 (later No 25324) heads north up the 1 in 100 of the 'Long Drag' north of Horton-in-Ribblesdale returning home with the Carlisle breakdown train, the red livery of the latter contrasting with the locomotive's rather drab all-over blue. No D7674 was only a few months old when this picture was taken on 28 October 1967, having been delivered from Derby in blue livery earlier that year. It is interesting to note that this was one of the 18 locomotives originally to have been built by Beyer Peacock at Gorton, the work only going to Derby Loco Works when the private contractor found itself unable to complete the original order because of looming insolvency.
Barrie Walker
Leica M2 Kodachrome II

Right: No D5256 takes the 'Little North Western' line at Settle Junction with a fine 11-coach rake of mainly ex-LMS and ex-LNER coaches forming a Leeds-Morecambe express on 22 July 1967. Although the Class 25s were strong engines, a train such as this would present quite a formidable challenge to a Type 2 diesel on express timings, as demonstrated by the thick exhaust that the locomotive is emitting at this point. It is worth speculating on whether cross-country rail travel has really progressed in the 22 years since this picture was taken. The same journey today would be undertaken in a Class 144 diesel multiple-unit — 70 miles in little more than a bus! *Barrie Walker*
Leica M2 Kodachrome II

Left: The Carnforth-Settle Junction line threads glorious scenery and to this day is a favourite for traction photographers. Epitomising the nature of the line is this view of two Sulzer Type 2s, led by No D5147, crossing Clapham viaduct on 14 June 1968 with a rake of eastbound mineral wagons. Besides the freight traffic, the Leeds-Morecambe locomotive-hauled services were for many years entrusted to the Sulzers. *Roger Bastin*
Retina Reflex 3 Kodachrome II

Above: Gorton-built No D7629 (later No 25279), still carrying two-tone green livery, leads Derby-built No D5219 (to become No 25069) into Leamington Spa with a heavy up permanent way train in October 1973. No 25069 ended its days on exhibition train duty, touring the country with the 'Travel Key' promotional train, before being taken out of service in December 1983. No 25279 was luckier, being one of the last of the class to be withdrawn. Its BR career finished at Wigan Springs

Branch on 18 March 1987 and the locomotive is now to be found preserved on the Llangollen Railway. *Bryan Hicks*
Pentax S1A Agfa CT18 1/250, f5

17

Above Derby Works was very much the home of the 'baby Sulzers'. The lion's share were built there and, with the exception of the Scottish locomotives, all returned to the works for classified overhauls. On 14 August 1971 four examples were present in this view of the erecting shop. These included No D5016 from the original pilot order Derby build, and No D5218 from the second batch of 1,250bhp Class 25 variants. Interestingly the latter sports blue livery, but with small yellow warning panels and the lion & wheel emblem. *William H. Dady Leica 111G 35mm Summaron Kodachrome II*

Above: Nos D7595 and D7597 pass Torside on the lamented Woodhead route with a football excursion on 14 March 1970. Manchester United were playing at Sheffield and the other specials produced a Class 40, a '45', and a '50'! No D7597, later to become No 25247, was the last locomotive constructed with front gangway doors. Air horns were mounted on the roof adjacent to the route indicator boxes on this batch.
Gavin Morrison
Pentax SP1000 50mm Takumar Kodachrome II

Left: No D5115 approaches Stonehaven with the down mail from Carstairs on 9 July 1966. Built by BR at Derby in 1960, it was withdrawn 16 years later in December 1976, finally being scrapped at Swindon in June 1977. *Roger Bastin*
Retina Reflex 3 Kodachrome II 1/500, f2.8

Above: A total of 19 Type 2s, Nos D5114-32, were built at Derby in 1960 for use in Scotland, although it is perhaps the BRCW designs (later Classes 26 and 27) that have enjoyed the strongest association with routes north of the Border. Several locomotives were fitted with automatic tablet catching equipment for working over single lines signalled under the Electric Token Block system. In this view, taken at Kyle of Lochalsh on Saturday 5 September 1973, an unidentified Class 24, with gangway doors sealed against draughts and tablet catcher recess just visible on the cabside, stands with a Class 26 following arrival with the 07.05 mixed train from Dingwall. In their latter years, most Scottish locomotives were fitted with sealed beam headlights for use when working over remote lines with ungated level crossings.
David C. Rodgers
Pentax SP500 Kodachrome II 1/125, f5.6

21

Left: Midlands freight duties were always a preserve of the Class 25s, their Bo-Bo wheel arrangement making them suitable for shunting in yards where the trackwork is not always of the highest standard — indeed, many London Midland Region drivers feel that their Class 31 replacements are weaker engines and more prone to derailments in such circumstances. In this view, No 25213 chugs out of Toton Yard with a short train of HAA coal wagons on 24 April 1985. Delivered new from Derby 20 years earlier, this locomotive became something of a celebrity in 1987, being one of only 15 Class 25s to remain in service beyond the official 15 March withdrawal deadline. The locomotive finally succumbed at Carlisle on 19 March, but not before coming to the aid of a failed Lancaster-Leeds DMU during the previous week and hauling it onwards from Carnforth! *Ian Gould*
Pentax 6×7 105mm Takumar Agfa R100S 1/250, f8

Above: This view shows No 25245 in charge of a southbound continental van train near Ryecroft Junction, Walsall. Built as No D7595 at Darlington, No 25245 saw numerous allocations during its existence including, unusually, Wellingborough. At the time of this photograph, 24 July 1978, it was a Bescot locomotive and thus on home territory.
Michael Mensing
Bronica S2A Agfachrome 50S 1/800, f5

Above: Derby-built No 25223 (formerly No D7573) became a Western Region locomotive in October 1971 when it was allocated to Plymouth Laira. It stayed there until withdrawal in October 1980 and was broken up immediately at Swindon Works. This March 1977 view illustrates the locomotive shunting at the cider factory at Whimple on the former Southern Region main line to Exeter. *Peter Doel Nikon F2A Ektachrome 200*

Right: Class 25/2 No 25143 bursts into the sunshine at Ambergate, on the Midland main line, with an up train of vans on 15 August 1978. At this time the majority of such workings were entrusted to the BR-Sulzer Type 2s, although 'Peak' Type 4s were generally employed on the heavier services. *Les Nixon Leica M3 135mm Summicron Kodachrome 25 1/500, f2.8*

Left: No 25036 passes Guiseley Junction at Shipley near Bradford with the up morning Glasgow-Nottingham service on 27 November 1978. The usual motive power was a Class 45 or 47 and the 'baby Sulzer' would have struggled to keep time over the Settle & Carlisle with its six-coach load.
Gavin Morrison
Pentax SP1000 85mm Takumar Kodachrome 25 1/250, f3.5

Above: Main line duty for No 25060; the photogenic station of York provides the setting as the locomotive waits to take the 20.23 service to Liverpool on 5 January 1983. In 1980 this machine was transferred to Cardiff and, later, was one of the regular performers on the Cambrian line. Its original identity was as No D5210, a Derby product of 1963 vintage. Sent to Doncaster Works for scrapping (in working order), the locomotive was

one of those then stored at Goole before being sent to the Leicester yard of Vic Berry Ltd. *Barry Plues*
Pentax SP1000 Ektachrome 200 10sec, f5.6

Right: Spent nuclear fuel traffic has ensured the future for the Blaenau Ffestiniog-Trawsfynydd line and provided the Class 25s with work until their demise in 1987. Gunpowder traffic from Maentwrog Road station on the same section of line has also been a Class 25 duty. No 25258 brings a nuclear flask train from Trawsfynydd into Blaenau on the ex-GWR line en route to Sellafield. The date was 12 August 1983. *Les Nixon*
Pentax 6×7 Ektachrome 200 1/250, f5.6

Left: The Cumbrian Coast line, from Barrow-in-Furness to Carlisle, is not often photographed, but this superb vista shows the rewards that can be reaped by the diligent photographer. With the foothills of the Lake District in the background, No 25232 trundles a Carnforth-Workington freight across Eskmeals viaduct, just south of Ravenglass, on 4 September 1979. *David C. Rodgers*
Pentax SP500 Kodachrome 25 1/250, f3.5

Above: An interesting pairing of Class 25/3 No 25325 and Class 47/0 No 47280 powers the 12.35 Severn Tunnel Junction-Mossend freight at Magor, in South Wales, on 26 November 1984. Classes 24 and 25 were equipped for multiple working under the Blue Star system, but the Class 47s were not, with the result that this formation would have been worked in tandem, with a driver in each locomotive.

Geoff Cann
Pentax MX 55mm Takumar Kodachrome 64
1/500, f4

Right: Derby-built No 25052 shunts at Hayle Quay on 9 October 1980. This was one of its final duties, for the locomotive was condemned in the same month and by the end of the year had been scrapped at Swindon Works. No 25052 had been transferred to the Western Region as long ago as 1971 serving at Bristol until May 1973 and thereafter until its demise at Plymouth Laira. *Hugh Dady*
Praktica 1V 50mm Tessar Kodachrome 64
1/200, f8

Left: An embankment covered with summer daisies provides a foil to No 25161 slogging northbound away from Tunstead towards Great Rocks Junction with 6F44, the 17.45 Tunstead-Oakleigh on 7 July 1983. The majority of services to and from this extensive limestone quarrying area are now handled by Railfreight Sector Class 37/5s. *Paul D. Shannon Olympus OM1 50mm Zuiko Kodachrome 64 1/250, f5.6*

Above: You can almost hear the spluttering exhaust note echoing off the Derbyshire hills as this unidentified Class 25 struggles up the gradient approaching Chinley North signalbox with a lengthy train of ICI bogie hoppers bound for Tunstead on 27 May 1977. The 25s were always at home hauling freight trains, where the relatively low gearing gave them an advantage, but use on heavy services which required sustained full-power running put a considerable strain on the AEI traction motors, the frequent failure of which was one of the factors which prevented the 25s from achieving target levels of reliability, particularly in later years. *Les Nixon Leica M3 Kodachrome 25*

Left: Northenden cement terminal on 28 May 1985; loaded CPV wagons are shunted by Nos 25051 and 25200 before the locomotives return a rake of empties to Earles cement works at Hope. This service runs twice weekly in summer and thrice weekly in winter. Both are Derby-built machines, No 25051 emerging in 1963 as No D5201 and 25200 making its debut in 1965 as No D7550.
Paul D. Shannon
Olympus OM1 Kodachrome 64 1/250, f5.6-8

Above: The Earles cement works at Hope has long provided business for the Class 25s and on 27 January 1979 it was the turn of No 25308 for rostered duty. A Midlands lines locomotive when brand-new as No D7658 in August 1966, this locomotive had numerous transfers of allocation during its life. *Les Nixon*
Leica M2 Kodachrome 25 1/250, f4

39

Left: The Class 25/3 sub-class was built in 1965-67 and was visually almost identical to the later batch of Class 25/2 locomotives. None of this sub-class was fitted with train heating equipment and consequently appearances on passenger work were not common. Performing typical work at Millerhill is No 25258, seen here leaving the departures side of the yard with the 18.40 fitted freight to Perth on 14 June 1982. In order to avoid having to pass through Edinburgh the train would have taken the freight route from Niddrie South Junction to Haymarket West Junction, thereby skirting the south of the city.
Mrs D. A. Robinson
Pentax 6×7 150mm Takumar
Ektachrome 200 1/500, f5.6

Right: Passing through the splendid scenery of the Lune Gorge, No 25269 heads south near Tebay with the Dalston-Stanlow empty oil tanks on the afternoon of 1 March 1986. One month later, on 2 April, the locomotive was withdrawn at Carlisle Kingmoor depot. It was a Scottish machine when brand new as No 7619, and during its two decades of service was allocated predominantly in the Midlands either at Toton or Bescot. *Peter J. Robinson*
Pentax 6×7 Ektachrome 200 1/1000, f6.3

Left: Class 25/2 No 25141 heads a southbound unfitted freight at Staveley on 20 September 1979 in a picture full of railway interest. The line just visible in the foreground led to Seymour Yard and Markham Colliery, but was lifted in the mid-1980s. Trains such as this, with braking supplied by the locomotive and brakevan only, required careful handling, and keeping the speed below the 25mph limit for such workings could place considerable strain on the traction motors. *Les Nixon Nikon F 85mm Nikkor Kodachrome 25 1/250 f4.2*

Right: Melton Mowbray is rather unfairly best known to many people as the home of the pork pie, but the cross-country Peterborough-Leicester route on which the town is situated carries enough interesting traffic to satisfy most enthusiasts. With springtime buds adding some colour to the scene, Class 25/3 No 25254 is seen east of the station with an empty cement train bound for Ketton cement works on 25 April 1984. At this time No 25254 had nearly three years left in service, being withdrawn at Crewe on 4 September 1986. *Rodney A. Lissenden Pentax 6×7 150mm Takumar Agfa CT18 1/500, f4*

Above: Class 25 No 25192, heads a Northampton-Bescot Speedlink service past the National Exhibition Centre at Birmingham International on 27 April 1984. The end came for this locomotive on 7 May 1986. *Chris Milner*
Canon AE1 Fuji 100 1/250, f5.6

Right: Using their combined 2,500hp to the full, Class 25/1 Nos 25037 and 25051 storm away from Hooton South, on the now-electrified GW-LNW Birkenhead Joint Line, with 6V32, the 14.53 Ellesmere Port-Severn Tunnel Junction block bitumen tankers, on 8 June 1984. Note the fine LNWR signalbox and the lattice-post signal gantry in the background, both sadly now demolished. Both these locomotives were built at Derby in 1963. *Andrew Bannister*
Olympus OM1n 135mm Zuiko Kodachrome 64 1/250, f6.3

Left: Nos 25202 and 25119 approach Machynlleth with the 07.35 Euston-Aberystwyth on 30 July 1983. The Class 25s took over the summer Saturday Cambrian turns from the Class 24s and became a familiar sight double heading these heavy trains. This trip was uneventful, but 1983 was a poor year for Cambrian punctuality. Many of the locomotives rostered by Bescot for these workings were hardly fit to descend Talerddig bank let alone tackle the climb back up it. Matters were much improved by the following summer which was to be the last year when Class 25s worked these services.
Mike Robinson
Pentax MX 50mm Takumar Kodachrome 64 1/500, f4

Above: Class 25 locomotives were used to launch the locomotive-hauled Crewe-Cardiff service back in 1977, taking over from the inadequate Class 120 and 123 DMUs previously employed, and these trains were solid Class 25 turns until the use of eth stock saw the 'Rats' usurped by Class 33s in May 1981. The attractive Border country at Marshbrook sees the passage of Class 25/1 No 25027 with the 16.02 Crewe-Cardiff on 5 September 1980.
Hugh Dady
Praktica IV 50mm Tessar Kodachrome 64 1/200, f5.6

49

Left: The condition of structures on the Cambrian lines is such that only rolling stock with a route availability of RA5 or less is permitted on the line except with special authority. The Class 25s fitted into this category, and this made them ideal for working the summer Saturday Euston-Aberystwyth trains onwards from Wolverhampton. The takeover of these services by Class 37s in 1985 largely spelt the end of Class 25-hauled passenger turns but an exception was this LNER Society excursion to Aberystwyth, seen here at Dovey Junction in the care of Nos 25058 and 25078 on 6 May 1985. This was the first locomotive-hauled passenger train to Aberystwyth that year, and had taken the Abbey Foregate curve at Shrewsbury thereby avoiding the customary reversal.
John Cowburn
Pentax MX   50mm
Kodachrome 64   1/125, f5.6-8

Right: In this busy scene front coach enthusiasts savour Nos 25193 and 25282 on the 10.10 Aberystwyth-Euston hammering out of Shrewsbury past Abbey Foregate, whose signalbox still controls a number of lower quadrant signals, many of which are on wooden posts and date from GWR days. On the left another pair of 'Rats' await a path through the station with a northbound tanker train. The date of the picture is 1 September 1984.
Hugh Ballantyne
Leica M3   135mm Summicron
Kodachrome 25   1/500, f2.8

Below: In recent years the only diagrammed freight working on the Cambrian lines has been the Stanlow-Aberystwyth and return Shell company train, and this was a regular Class 25 turn until their demise brought pairs of Class 20s to the line. The scenic location of Carno is the setting for Class 25/3 No 25288 with 7F79, the return 15.30 (Wednesdays only) Aberystwyth-Stanlow on 17 September 1986. *Geoff Bannister*
Olympus OM1n 85mm Zuiko Kodachrome 64 1/500, f4.5

Left: The 'Rats' were once a common sight scuttling around the freight yards of London. On 14 March 1985 Nos 25265 and 25212 make their way from Willesden Brent sidings to South West yard to pick up a train of empty car carriers. *Hugh Dady Nikkormat FT2 85mm Nikkor Kodachrome 64 1/500, f3.5*

Right: This pair of Class 25/2s, Nos 25190 and 25176, are assured a leisurely day's work at the head of a lengthy permanent way train at Kensal Green Junction on 31 March 1985. The engineers had taken possession of the site in order to allow the remodelling of the junction layout, an operation which involved the use of Plasser & Theurer crane No 81526 visible on the right-hand side of the picture. Class 25s were an every-day sight in northwest London for more than 20 years but by the time this picture was taken they were becoming less common in the area. *Hugh Dady Nikkormat FT2 50mm Nikkor Kodachrome 64 1/250, f5.6*

Above: Class 25/2 No 25191 disturbs the peace at Prestatyn, on the North Wales coast line, with a train of sulphur from Mostyn Dock to Amlwch on 5 March 1986. Another lingering survivor of the class, No 25191 ironically performed its very last duty in BR service over this line, a Llandudno Junction-Crewe Gresty Green permanent way train on 16 March 1987. Thankfully, this locomotive can now be savoured in action on the North Yorkshire Moors Railway. *Larry Goddard*
Olympus OM1 100mm Zuiko Kodachrome 64 1/500, f4

Right: With their BR days drawing rapidly to a close, the remaining '25s' were often found pottering around the lines of North Wales. A favourite trip was 7T91 conveying explosives from Maentwrog Road siding, serving the factory at Penrhyndeudraeth, to Llandudno Junction. Retirement is just 11 days away as No 25912 *Tamworth Castle* rounds the curve at Roman Bridge on 12 March 1987 amid the glorious scenery of Snowdonia. *Andrew Bannister*
Olympus OM1n 50mm Zuiko Kodachrome 64 1/250, f5.6

Right: How to survive — become a Research Division locomotive! This course of events has been the salvation for several locomotives whose sisters have gone to the scrapyard. After an eventful revenue-earning career, embracing such depots as March, Willesden, Rugby, Finsbury Park, Haymarket, Longsight and Crewe, No 24061, formerly No D5061, was 'Departmentalised' in 1975 with No TDB968007. In 1978, the Research Division, Derby, assumed responsibility and it became No 97201, decked out in the Research Division livery, and later named *Experiment*. Its usual role was to haul the Tribometer train and it was on this duty when photographed at Bradbury on the East Coast main line on 3 April 1984 during one of several sorties on the line. *Neil Simpson*
Pentax ME Agfachrome CT21 1/500, f5.6

Left: The advent of the Mk 3 sleeper resulted in a strange reprieve for three Class 25s. They were converted into train heating units and used on the Glasgow-Fort William line, being hauled as part of the train formation. The three machines were given Departmental numbers of 97250-3 and dubbed ETHEL (Electric Train Heat Ex-Locomotive). When the electric train heat-fitted Class 37/4 series locomotives came on stream, the ETHELs became redundant, except for occasional static train heating duties. A requirement for testing Mk 3 sleepers in Derby Litchurch Lane Works resulted in No 97250 being transferred for this purpose. It is pictured en route to Derby from Eastfield, Glasgow, pausing at Gateshead depot on 30 November 1986.
Peter J. Robinson
Pentax 6×7 Ektachrome 200 1/125, f8

Right: ETHEL 3, alias No 97253, formerly No 25314, ex-D7664 (any more?!) was the first ETHEL required for extended use. A decision to cease using the steam heating equipment on the coaching stock used for steam hauled specials (due to lack of testing equipment) meant that this machine was brought up from Scotland to Marylebone where it was put to use on the 'Shakespeare Limited' trains to Stratford-upon-Avon. Its first run was at the end of 1986, and in the spring of 1987 ETHEL 3 was repainted into InterCity livery. It is seen at Stratford being shunted by Class 47 No 47432 on 22 March 1987.
Bill Sharman
Mamiya 645   Ektachrome 100   1/500, f8-11

Left: No D7535 *Mercury* prepares to leave Kingswear for Paignton with the return 'Sundowner' evening excursion on 29 July 1987. Delivered from Derby in 1965, No D7535, later to become No 25185, was always a Midland engine and was finally condemned at Toton on 5 November 1984. While sisters were towed away for scrap No 25185 remained at the depot for apprentice training. When offered for preservation there were several bids, the successful one coming from the Torbay & Dartmouth Railway. The locomotive arrived at Paignton in February 1986 and was put to work that summer. In early 1987 No D7535 was

repainted into original two-tone green. For the purist the pale green shade is not quite correct and the numbers should be in the squarer style (see page 7) but for all this the locomotive looks most attractive. Hopefully the headcode blinds will be reinstated in the future. *Mark Wilkins*
Hasselblad 2000 FCM Ektachrome Pro 100
1/125, f5.6

Above: Nos D5054 and D5209 approach Oakworth with an afternoon Keighley-Oxenhope working during the K&WVR diesel weekend on 6 November 1988. No D5054 was on loan from the

East Lancashire Railway at Bury where restoration was undertaken. Condemned from BR as surplus in July 1976, the locomotive saw re-use as a train heating generator on both the Western and Eastern regions. It was finally retired at the end of 1982 and moved to Bury in October 1983. No D5209, formerly No 25059 (see page 54), was delivered new from Derby in June 1963. It was one of those locomotives transferred to the WR in the 1970s before returning north where it was to last until the very end of Class 25 operation. *Mike Taylor*
Fuji 100 1/250, f5.6

Above: The evening sun begins to go down on the Class 25s. This was Hertfordshire Railtours' 100th tour and incorporated a pair of Class 25/9 'Rats' for this sub-class' first and last official railtour duty. The tour ran on 28 September 1986 and was titled 'The Mersey Ratcatcher'. Nos 25904 and 25910 were the chosen traction, seen here approaching Helsby Junction. *D. R. Johnson*
Mamiya 645 Agfa 100RS